MW00477013

Happiness Is...

Happiness Is . . .

Scripture text taken from The Holy Bible, New King James Version. Copyright © 1979, 1980, 1982 by Thomas Nelson, Inc.

Library of Congress Cataloging-in-Publication Data:
Happiness is—.
p. cm.
ISBN 0-8499-5158-5
1. Happiness—Religious aspects—Christianity—Quotations, maxims, etc.
2. Happiness—Biblical teaching.
BV4647.J68H36 1995
242—dc20
95-19188
CIP

WORD PUBLISHING
Dallas • London • Vancouver • Melbourne

For the Christian, happiness
is not dependent on circumstances.

∞

*Not that I speak in regard to need, for I have learned
in whatever state I am, to be content.*
PHILIPPIANS 4:11

*T*he Bible says that
happiness is doing the will of God.

∾

If you know these things,
blessed are you if you do them.
JOHN 13:17

*T*he hour we spend alone with God
is the most rewarding hour in the day.

You will show me the path of life;
in Your presence is fullness of joy; at Your
right hand are pleasures forevermore.
PSALM 16:11

$\mathcal{W}$e need look no further than Jesus
for an example of the joy of sacrifice.

∾

*Looking unto Jesus, the author and finisher
of our faith, who for the joy that was set before
Him endured the cross, despising the shame, and has
sat down at the right hand of the throne of God.*
HEBREWS 12:2

$\mathcal{S}$ome people bring a smile to
our lips every time we think of them.
They are a constant blessing.

*I thank my God upon every remembrance
of you, always in every prayer of mine making
request for you all with joy.*
PHILIPPIANS 1:3-4

*J*esus is not interested in our being simply happy; He wants us to be outrageously joyful!

∾

These things I have spoken to you,
that My joy may remain in you,
and that your joy may be full.
JOHN 15:11

*T*here is no joy to compare
with the joy of trusting Jesus as Savior.

∾

Whom having not seen you love.
Though now you do not see Him,
yet believing, you rejoice with joy
inexpressible and full of glory.
1 PETER 1:8

*C*hristians can rejoice
during times of trouble
because they know God uses
difficult circumstances to build
and strengthen character.

*My brethren, count it all joy
when you fall into various trials, . . .*
JAMES 1:2

*C*hristians not only
enjoy the joy of Jesus,
they enjoy Jesus Himself.

Rejoice in the Lord always.
Again I will say, rejoice!
PHILIPPIANS 4:4

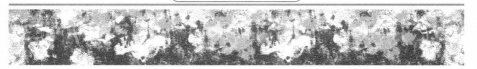

Jesus intends for us
to have the richest life imaginable.
The Christian never misses out.

I have come that they may have life,
and that they may have it more abundantly.
JOHN 10:10

*T*he Holy Spirit
is the wind under our wings
and the spring in our step.

*But those who wait on the LORD shall
renew their strength; they shall mount up
with wings like eagles, they shall run and not
be weary, they shall walk and not faint.*
ISAIAH 40:31

*W*hatever knocks life may bring,
Christians can smile—because they are
on the victory side.

Yet in all these things
we are more than conquerors
through Him who loved us.
ROMANS 8:37

*I*f you have the joy of Jesus,
your face will show it.

*A merry heart
makes a cheerful countenance, . . .*
PROVERBS 15:13

$\mathcal{J}$esus is our constant
companion in this life,
and His face will be
the first we see in eternity.

*Lo, I am with you always,
even to the end of the age.*
MATTHEW 28:20

No matter how threatening
the circumstances of life,
God is in control.

But as for you,
you meant evil against me;
but God meant it for good.
GENESIS 50:20

*W*e can rest assured
God always loves us.
The Holy Spirit gives us
this assurance.

Now hope does not disappoint,
because the love of God has been poured out
in our hearts by the Holy Spirit
who was given to us.
ROMANS 5:5

𝒫rayer is a key to happiness.
When we pray, God lifts our burdens
and grants us peace.

Be anxious for nothing, but in everything
by prayer and supplication, with thanksgiving,
let your requests be made known to God;
and the peace of God, which surpasses
all understanding, will guard your hearts
and minds through Christ Jesus.
PHILIPPIANS 4:6-7

*I*f we come to God
with nothing in our hands,
He will fill them
with all the riches of heaven.

∞

Blessed are the poor in spirit,
for theirs is the kingdom of heaven.
MATTHEW 5:3

*W*hat the world calls happiness
is only temporary pleasure.
It doesn't satisfy, and it always
produces regrets.

[Moses,] choosing rather to suffer affliction
with the people of God than to enjoy
the passing pleasures of sin.
HEBREWS 11:25

*C*hristians are a happy people
who spontaneously break out in song.
No wonder—they serve a God
who does the same.

∾

The LORD your God in your midst,
the Mighty One, will save; He will rejoice over you
with gladness, He will quiet you in His love,
He will rejoice over you with singing.
ZEPHANIAH 3:17

*G*od has a wonderful
plan for each of our lives.
We have but to obey Him
to get in on it.

For I know the thoughts that
I think toward you, says the LORD,
thoughts of peace and not of evil,
to give you a future and a hope.
JEREMIAH 29:11

*C*hristians are incurable optimists.
They know the power of the One
who dwells within them.

∾

*I can do all things through Christ
who strengthens me.*
PHILIPPIANS 4:13

*I*t is exciting to see God
work sovereignly in our lives.
We cannot help but celebrate.

This is the day the LORD has made;
we will rejoice and be glad in it.
PSALM 118:24

Our God is a good God,
and He is good to us. He protects us,
and we are ever on His mind.

The LORD is good,
a stronghold in the day of trouble;
and He knows those who trust in Him.
NAHUM 1:7

$\mathscr{N}$ever let fear rob you
of the joy that is rightfully yours.
Let the Holy Spirit give you courage
and encouragement.

∾

For God has not given us a spirit of fear,
but of power and of love and of a sound mind.
2 TIMOTHY 1:7

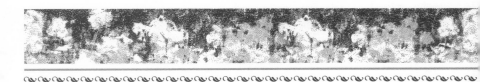

$\mathcal{O}$ur Lord goes before us,
like a shepherd with his sheep,
to ensure that all of our needs are met.

∾

The LORD is my shepherd;
I shall not want.
PSALM 23:1

$\mathcal{P}$eace and joy come
from knowing the victorious,
risen Christ.

∾

These things I have spoken to you,
that in Me you may have peace.
In the world you will have tribulation;
but be of good cheer, I have overcome the world.
JOHN 16:33

$\mathcal{B}$elievers can
throw their shoulders back
and hold their heads high.
Wherever they go, the Creator
of the universe goes with them.

Have I not commanded you?
Be strong and of good courage; do not be afraid,
nor be dismayed, for the LORD your God is with you
wherever you go.
JOSHUA 1:9

$\mathscr{T}$he secret of happiness
is to enjoy the day God has given you;
leave tomorrow in His hands.

∾

Therefore do not worry about tomorrow,
for tomorrow will worry about its own things.
MATTHEW 6:34

$\mathcal{T}$hink about all the blessings
God has brought into your life,
and you will sing out in praise!

Bless the LORD, O my soul,
and forget not all His benefits.
PSLAM 103:2

*W*hat a blessed relief you will feel
if you let Jesus carry your load.
You matter to Him.

*Casting all your care upon Him,
for He cares for you.*
1 PETER 5:7

$\mathcal{W}$e can rest in the knowledge
that God is able to handle any situation
and any person.

But Jesus looked at them and said to them,
"With men this is impossible, but with God
all things are possible."
MATTHEW 19:26

*I*f you want to be happy,
pay attention to God's Word
and trust Him.

∾

He who heeds the word wisely will find good,
and whoever trusts in the Lord, happy is he.
PROVERBS 16:20

$\mathcal{H}$appiness is not something
we create; it is something
the Holy Spirit produces in us.

But the fruit of the Spirit
is love, joy, peace, . . .
GALATIANS 5:22

$\mathcal{W}$hether you are down or up,
pray and praise your way through life.

Is anyone among you suffering?
Let him pray. Is any one cheerful?
Let him sing psalms.
JAMES 5:13

$\mathcal{A}$ sunny disposition is good
for your health.

∾

A merry heart does good,
like medicine, . . .
PROVERBS 17:22

*D*on't pursue happiness,
pursue God and His will for your life;
then happiness will follow.

*But seek first the kingdom of God
and His righteousness, and all these things
shall be added to you.*
MATTHEW 6:33

$\mathcal{H}$appiness doesn't come
from merely hearing God's Word,
but from doing it.

∾

But He said, " . . . blessed are those
who hear the word of God and keep it!"
LUKE 11:28

*G*od reserves a special blessing
for those who show compassion
to the needy.

∽

He who despises his neighbor sins;
but he who has mercy on the poor, happy is he.
PROVERBS 14:21

Some people think happiness
comes from holding on to what they have.
Jesus says it comes from giving
what we have to Him.

For whoever desires to save his life will lose it,
and whoever loses his life for My sake will find it.
MATTHEW 16:25

*G*odly people pass an inheritance
of happiness on to their children—
the happiness that comes from having
a godly mom or dad.

The righteous man walks in his integrity;
his children are blessed after him.
PROVERBS 20:7

*C*hristians are happy
doing the will of God,
because His desires
have become their desires.

*Delight yourself also in the LORD,
and He shall give you the desires of your heart.*
PSALM 37:4

God gives us
the simple pleasures of life
as blessings to enjoy.

∾

I know that there is nothing better for them
than to rejoice, and to do good in their lives,
and also that every man should eat and drink
and enjoy the good of all his labor;
it is the gift of God.
ECCLESIASTES 3:12-13

$\mathcal{W}$hether we mourn
over our sins or over other heartaches,
God comes alongside to cheer us up.

∾

Blessed are those who mourn,
for they shall be comforted.
MATTHEW 5:4

*E*veryone enjoys receiving a gift.
The greatest gift is eternal life.

∽

*Every good gift
and every perfect gift is from above,
and comes down from the Father of lights,
with whom there is no variation
or shadow of turning.*
JAMES 1:17

*A*lways, everywhere,
under all circumstances,
we are to be cheerful.

Rejoice always, . . .
1 THESSALONIANS 5:16

*W*hy should we worry
about our needs? We can rest secure
knowing that God will always meet them.

∼

And my God shall supply all your need
according to His riches in glory by Christ Jesus.
PHILIPPIANS 4:19

*I*f we look at circumstances,
we can become afraid.
When we look to God,
our fears melt away.

∾

You will keep him in perfect peace,
whose mind is stayed on You,
because he trusts in You.
ISAIAH 26:3

$\mathcal{T}$rue peace of mind comes
from trusting a trustworthy God.

∾

What then shall we say to these things?
If God is for us, who can be against us?
ROMANS 8:31

*T*here is no joy to compare with
new life in Christ. Sins are forgiven,
and life will never be the same.

*Therefore, if anyone is in Christ, he is
a new creation; old things have passed away;
behold, all things have become new.*
2 CORINTHIANS 5:17

*H*umility is a key to happiness.
When we are humble, we are
yielded to God's will.

*Take My yoke upon you and learn
from Me, for I am gentle and lowly in heart,
and you will find rest for your souls.*
MATTHEW 11:29

$\mathcal{K}$eep your life free from sin
and your mind saturated with the Word
of God; happiness will surely follow.

∾

Blessed is the man who walks not in the counsel
of the ungodly, nor stands in the path of sinners, . . .
but his delight is in the law of the LORD, and in His law
he meditates day and night.
PSALM 1:1, 2

God's children delight
to hear His voice speaking
through the pages of Scripture.

∿

Your words were found, and I ate them,
and Your word was to me the joy and rejoicing
of my heart; for I am called by Your name,
O LORD God of hosts.
JEREMIAH 15:16

$\mathcal{W}$e rejoice in the wonder of His creation.
The beauty and complexity of nature
reveal God's wisdom.

∾

*For You, LORD, have made me glad
through Your work; I will triumph in the works
of Your hands. O LORD, how great are Your works!
Your thoughts are very deep.*
PSALM 92:4-5

*T*he one longing
that will always be satisfied
is the longing for holiness.

∾

Blessed are those who hunger and thirst
for righteousness, for they shall be filled.
MATTHEW 5:6

*W*e don't deserve God's daily blessings,
but we get to enjoy them anyway.

∾

Through the LORD's mercies we are not consumed,
because His compassions fail not. They are new
every morning; great is Your faithfulness.
LAMENTATIONS 3:22-23

$\mathcal{W}$e can rejoice
that we are going to heaven.

∾

*Nevertheless do not rejoice in this,
that the spirits are subject to you, but rather rejoice
because your names are written in heaven.*
LUKE 10:20

$\mathcal{H}$ow happy we can be
if we have friends and family
who will be there for us
when the going gets rough.

A friend loves at all times,
and a brother is born for adversity.
PROVERBS 17:17

*W*hile angels in heaven
do not need to repent, they rejoice
over those who do; and so should we!

*Likewise, I say to you, there is joy
in the presence of the angels of God
over one sinner who repents.*
LUKE 15:10

$\mathcal{H}$appiness is a state
of mind. Think godly thoughts,
and you will experience godly joy.

∾

Finally, brethren, whatever things are true,
whatever things are noble, whatever things are just,
whatever things are pure, whatever things are lovely,
whatever things are of good report . . .
meditate on these things.
PHILIPPIANS 4:8

*I*f you help the hurting,
you will be happy.

Be kindly affectionate to one another
with brotherly love, in honor giving
preference to one another; . . .
ROMANS 12:10

It is hard to be happy
when you harbor hatred
in your heart.

∾

Let all bitterness, wrath, anger, clamor,
and evil speaking be put away from you. . . .
And be kind to one another, tenderhearted,
forgiving one another, even as God
in Christ also forgave you.
EPHESIANS 4:31-32

*W*hen we feel abandoned,
discouraged, and afraid,
God assures us of His love.
We can smile again.

∽

Fear not, for I am with you; be not dismayed,
for I am your God. I will strengthen you,
yes, I will help you, I will uphold you
with My righteous right hand.
ISAIAH 41:10

$\mathcal{Y}$ou don't need material things
to be happy if you have the Lord.

∾

*Let your conduct be without covetousness,
and be content with such things as you have.
For He Himself has said, "I will never leave you
nor forsake you."*
HEBREWS 13:5

*C*onfidence in God puts a song
in our heart and a smile on our lips.

∽

*And we know that all things work together for good
to those who love God, to those who are the called
according to His purpose.*
ROMANS 8:28

A person cannot sing praises to God
and remain unhappy.

I will sing to the LORD as long as I live;
I will sing praise to my God while I have my being.
PSALM 104:33

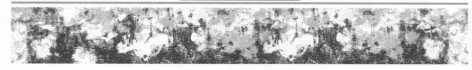

$\mathcal{P}$eople who spend time with God
show it on their faces;
they glow with His joy.

They looked to Him and were radiant,
and their faces were not ashamed.
PSALM 34:5

*I*f you lift another's load,
you will find your own is lighter.

∽

Blessed are the merciful,
for they shall obtain mercy.
MATTHEW 5:7

$\mathcal{T}$he world's joy glows brightly
for a moment and then fades away.
God's joy is forever!

∾

The ransomed of the LORD . . .
shall obtain joy and gladness;
sorrow and sighing shall flee away.
ISAIAH 51:11

*T*he happiest news ever brought to the ears of mankind was the announcement of the birth of the Savior.

Behold, I bring you good tidings of great joy which will be to all people. For there is born to you this day in the city of David a Savior, who is Christ the Lord.
LUKE 2:10-11

*C*hristians have every reason in
the world to get along with one another.
Harmony produces happiness.

∽

*Therefore if there is any consolation in Christ,
if any comfort of love, if any fellowship of the Spirit,
if any affection and mercy, fulfill my joy
by being like-minded, having the same love,
being of one accord, of one mind.*
PHILIPPIANS 2:1-2

$\mathcal{W}$hen you get Jesus,
you get everything
that makes a person happy.

∞

For He satisfies the longing soul,
and fills the hungry soul with goodness.
PSALM 107:9

$\mathcal{E}$njoy the joy of others.
Happiness is infectious.

Rejoice with those who rejoice, . . .
ROMANS 12:15

$\mathcal{E}$very good thing
God plans for His children
comes from knowing Jesus.

∽

Blessed be the God and Father of our Lord Jesus Christ,
who has blessed us with every spiritual blessing
in the heavenly places in Christ.
EPHESIANS 1:3

$\mathcal{W}$e obey God's commandments
because we love Him.
Walking in His will brings peace and joy.

∾

Blessed are those who keep His testimonies,
who seek Him with the whole heart!
PSALM 119:2

*T*here is no greater blessing
than knowing you are a child of God.

*The Spirit Himself
bears witness with our spirit
that we are children of God.*
ROMANS 8:16

$\mathcal{W}$e serve a superlative God
who delights in doing far more for us
than we could ever imagine.

∾

Now to Him who is able to do exceedingly abundantly
above all that we ask or think, according to the power
that works in us, to Him be glory. . . .
EPHESIANS 3:20-21

*W*hen we plant the seed
of the Word and water it with our tears,
God brings forth a harvest of souls.
We share in the joy of heaven.

∽

He who continually goes forth weeping,
bearing seed for sowing, shall doubtless come again
with rejoicing, bringing his sheaves with him.
PSALM 126:6

*T*here are honorable pleasures
that God means for us to enjoy
as gifts from His hand: a good meal
and a job well done.

∞

*It is good and fitting for one to eat and drink,
and to enjoy the good of all his labor in which he toils
under the sun all the days of his life
which God gives him.*
ECCLESIASTES 5:18

*A*ll the sufferings of this life
will one day pass away
just as surely as day follows night.

Weeping may endure for a night,
but joy comes in the morning.
PSALM 30:5

$\mathcal{M}$utual sacrifice and service
produce mutual joy—joy in serving Jesus
and in caring for one another.

Yes, and if I am being poured out
as a drink offering on the sacrifice and service
of your faith, I am glad and rejoice with you all.
For the same reason you also be glad and rejoice
with me.
PHILIPPIANS 2:17-18

$\mathcal{S}$in not only interrupts
our fellowship with God,
it distorts our vision of Him.

∾

*Blessed are the pure in heart,
for they shall see God.*
MATTHEW 5:8

Only holy hearts can see a holy God
and enjoy the beauty of His holiness.

∾

God is Spirit, and those who worship Him
must worship in spirit and truth.
JOHN 4:24

*T*he more self-absorbed we are,
the more dissatisfied we become.

∾

*Let each of you look out
not only for his own interests,
but also for the interests of others.*
PHILIPPIANS 2:4

*T*rue happiness does not come
from self-indulgence but from
selfless devotion to God.

∾

And I will say to my soul,
"Soul, you have many goods laid up for many years;
take your ease; eat, drink, and be merry."
But God said to him, "Fool! This night
your soul will be required of you."
LUKE 12:19-20

𝒩either worship nor service
should ever be drudgery.
God wants both to be pure joy,
an uplift to our spirits.

∽

Make a joyful shout to the LORD,
all you lands! Serve the LORD with gladness;
come before His presence with singing.
PSALM 100:1-2

$\mathcal{N}$othing can kill joy more quickly
than an unforgiving spirit.

Pursue peace with all people, . . .
lest any root of bitterness
springing up cause trouble.
HEBREWS 12:14-15

*I*f we could comprehend
all we have in Christ,
we would never stop rejoicing.

∾

That you may know what is the hope of His calling,
what are the riches of the glory of His inheritance
in the saints, and what is the exceeding greatness
of His power toward us who believe.
EPHESIANS 1:18-19

*T*o think that the Creator
of the universe is at work within us,
enabling us to choose and empowering us
to do His will, is awesome!

Work out your own salvation
with fear and trembling; for it is God who works
in you both to will and to do for His good pleasure.
PHILIPPIANS 2:12-13

*C*hristians are oases of hope
in a desert of despair; their souls
are continually fed by streams
of living water.

*Now may the God of hope fill you with all
joy and peace in believing, that you may abound
in hope by the power of the Holy Spirit.*
ROMANS 15:13

*C*hange a word,
change an attitude:
You don't *have* to give,
you *get* to give!

So let each one give as he purposes
in his heart, not grudgingly or of necessity;
for God loves a cheerful giver.
2 CORINTHIANS 9:7

God will banish all unhappiness
in the kingdom of heaven.

∾

*And God will wipe away every tear
from their eyes; there shall be no more death,
nor sorrow, nor crying. There shall be no more pain,
for the former things have passed away.*
REVELATION 21:4

$\mathcal{P}$eople are glad
when a good person succeeds.

∾

When the righteous rejoice,
there is great glory. . . .
PROVERBS 28:12

God blesses the nation
whose people honor Him
in their hearts.

*Blessed is the nation whose God is the LORD,
the people He has chosen as His own inheritance.*
PSALM 33:12

*T*he joy the wise men felt
at seeing the star was exceeded only
by the joy of seeing Jesus Himself.

∽

When they saw the star,
they rejoiced with exceedingly great joy.
And when they had come into the house,
they saw the young Child with Mary His mother,
and fell down and worshiped Him.
MATTHEW 2:10-11

$\mathcal{A}$ person with godly character
and a happy heart is wealthy indeed!

∾

*Now godliness with contentment
is great gain.*
1 TIMOTHY 6:6

$\mathcal{W}$hen leaders exhibit integrity,
people feel happy and secure.

*When the righteous are in authority,
the people rejoice.*
PROVERBS 29:2

*I*n a scary world,
the safest place to live
is close to God.

∾

He who dwells in the secret place
of the Most High shall abide under the shadow
of the Almighty. I will say of the LORD, "He is my refuge
and my fortress; my God, in Him I will trust."
PSALM 91:1-2

*T*he angels cheered
at the creation of the world.
Shouldn't we rejoice in its beauty?

*Where were you
when I laid the foundations of the earth? . . .
When the morning stars sang together,
and all the sons of God shouted for joy?*
JOB 38:4, 7

$\mathcal{T}$he sooner peace is restored
between ourselves and others,
the sooner happiness will return
to our hearts.

Blessed are the peacemakers,
for they shall be called sons of God.
MATTHEW 5:9

*W*hen a person is right with God,
the whole world seems a happy place.

For you shall go out with joy,
and be led out with peace; the mountains
and the hills shall break forth into singing
before you, and all the trees of the
field shall clap their hands.
ISAIAH 55:12

*J*esus' last prayer with His disciples
was about joy and comfort.

∾

But now I come to You,
and these things I speak in the world,
that they may have My joy
fulfilled in themselves.
JOHN 17:13

*H*appiness is freedom
from sin and guilt.

∾

And you shall know the truth,
and the truth shall make you free.
JOHN 8:32

$\mathcal{H}$appiness is a mind
renewed by Christ and a life lived
in conformity to His will.

Do not be conformed to this world,
but be transformed by the renewing of your mind,
that you may prove what is that good and acceptable
and perfect will of God.
ROMANS 12:2

*W*hen we trust Christ as our Savior,
we are covered by His righteousness.
God no longer sees our sin.
O happy day!

∽

*I will greatly rejoice in the LORD, my soul
shall be joyful in my God; for He has clothed
me with the garments of salvation, He has
covered me with the robe of righteousness.*
ISAIAH 61:10

*I*f we heed godly teaching
and follow godly examples,
God will grant us His peace.

*The things which you learned
and received and heard and saw in me,
these do, and the God of peace
will be with you.*
PHILIPPIANS 4:9

$\mathcal{O}$ne of the greatest joys
is to see others come
to know Christ as Savior.

*For what is our hope, or joy,
or crown of rejoicing? Is it not even you,
in the presence of our Lord Jesus Christ
at His coming?*
1 THESSALONIANS 2:19

*C*hrist has conquered
sin, death, and the grave;
we are the joyful trophies
of His triumph.

Now thanks be to God
who always leads us in triumph
in Christ, and through us diffuses
the fragrance of His knowledge
in every place.
2 CORINTHIANS 2:14

$\mathcal{W}$hen we stand before Jesus,
His approval of our faithfulness
will be our greatest reward.

∾

His lord said to him,
"Well done, good and faithful servant;
you have been faithful over a few things,
I will make you ruler over many things.
Enter into the joy of your lord."
MATTHEW 25:23

$\mathcal{H}$appiness is having
Jesus in our hearts and enjoying
intimate fellowship with Him.

Behold, I stand at the door and knock.
If anyone hears My voice and opens the door,
I will come in to him and dine with him,
and he with Me.
REVELATION 3:20

Christians have great
peace of mind because they know
that God will raise them up at the last
day and will call them by name.

But if anyone loves God,
this one is known by Him.
1 CORINTHIANS 8:3

*I*f something
is weighing on your conscience,
you will be miserable until you have made
the matter right with God and man.

*This being so, I myself always strive
to have a conscience without offense
toward God and men.*
ACTS 24:16

$\mathcal{L}$ike Jacob, persist in your faith
until God touches your life
with His hand of blessing.

And He said,
"Let Me go, for the day breaks."
But he said, "I will not let You go
unless You bless me!"
GENESIS 32:26

*W*e need not worry
about God's willingness to bless us.
It pleases Him to do so.

∾

Do not fear, little flock,
for it is your Father's good pleasure
to give you the kingdom.
LUKE 12:32

*I*f God did not withhold
the greatest blessing He could give us—
His Son—He will surely give us
every other blessing as well.

∾

He who did not spare
His own Son, but delivered Him up
for us all, how shall He not with Him
also freely give us all things?
ROMANS 8:32

*T*he Holy Spirit in our hearts
assures us that God loves us
and will carry out His plan
for our lives.

∾

You were sealed with the Holy Spirit
of promise, who is the guarantee
of our inheritance until the redemption
of the purchased possession.
EPHESIANS 1:13-14

$\mathcal{W}$e must step out in faith
to experience the blessings
God has in store for us.

Now the LORD had said to Abram:
"Get out of your country, from your family
and from your father's house, to a land that
I will show you. . . . I will bless you and make
your name great; and you shall be a blessing."
GENESIS 12:1-2

*G*od delights in answering prayer.
We do not have the peace and joy
we could have because we do not ask.

∽

Call to Me, and I will answer you,
and show you great and mighty things,
which you do not know.
JEREMIAH 33:3

$\mathcal{S}$aving faith brings so many blessings:
peace with God, grace to live,
and confidence about the future.
No wonder Christians have joy!

∞

Having been justified by faith, we have peace
with God through our Lord Jesus Christ,
through whom also we have access by faith
into this grace in which we stand, and rejoice
in hope of the glory of God.
ROMANS 5:1-2

*T*he more friends do for
each other, the deeper and more
satisfying their relationship.

❧

*Let the word of Christ dwell in
you richly in all wisdom, teaching and
admonishing one another in psalms and
hymns and spiritual songs, singing with
grace in your hearts to the Lord.*
COLOSSIANS 3:16

*T*o be happy, assume your own responsibilities. Don't shift them to someone else.

But let each one examine his own work, and then he will have rejoicing in himself alone, and not in another. For each one shall bear his own load.
GALATIANS 6:4-5

$\mathcal{T}$he joy of friendship
is in direct proportion to
the investment each friend
makes in the relationship.

*A man who has friends
must himself be friendly, . . .*
PROVERBS 18:24

$\mathscr{W}$e should rejoice if we
are counted worthy to suffer
for Christ's sake.

∞

Blessed are you
when they revile and persecute you,
and say all kinds of evil against you falsely
for My sake. Rejoice and be exceeding glad,
for great is your reward in heaven.
MATTHEW 5:11-12

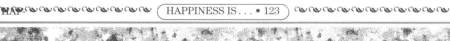

*T*he calm and serenity
that marked Jesus' life can be ours
as well. We have but to trust God
as He did.

∞

Peace I leave with you,
My peace I give to you; not as
the world gives do I give to you.
Let not your heart be troubled,
neither let it be afraid.
JOHN 14:27

$\mathcal{H}$appiness is not for sale.
Why waste your money on things
that do not satisfy?

Why do you spend money
for what is not bread, and your wages
for what does not satisfy? Listen diligently
to Me, and eat what is good, and let your soul
delight itself in abundance.
ISAIAH 55:2

*J*esus meets us at our point
of deepest need and satisfies
our deepest longings.

∾

But whoever drinks of the water
that I shall give him will never thirst.
But the water that I shall give him
will become in him a fountain of water
springing up into everlasting life.
JOHN 4:14

*C*hristians have
the satisfaction of knowing
that everything they do for Christ
counts and has eternal value.

∾

Therefore, my beloved brethren,
be steadfast, immovable, always abounding
in the work of the Lord, knowing that your labor
is not in vain in the Lord.
1 CORINTHIANS 15:58

*D*eath mocks
all human achievement.
Jesus' assurance of eternal life
provides the greatest hope
we can have.

*Jesus said to her, "I am the resurrection and the life.
He who believes in Me, though he may die, he shall live.
And whoever lives and believes in Me shall never die."*
JOHN 11:25-26

$\mathcal{T}$he happiness
we receive is in proportion
to the happiness we give.

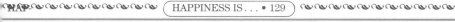

Give, and it will be given to you:
good measure, pressed down, shaken together,
and running over will be put into your bosom.
For with the same measure that you use,
it will be measured back to you.
LUKE 6:38

*J*esus replaces sorrow with joy, heaviness with happiness. He nailed the cause of all unhappiness to His cross.

He has sent Me to heal the brokenhearted . . .
to comfort all who mourn, . . . to give them beauty
for ashes, the oil of joy for mourning, the garment
of praise for the spirit of heaviness; . . .
ISAIAH 61:2-3

*I*f we want peace in our time,
we must storm heaven's gates
with our prayers.

*Therefore I exhort first of all
that supplications, prayers, intercessions,
and giving of thanks be made for all men,
for kings, and all who are in authority,
that we may lead a quiet and peaceable life
in all godliness and reverence.*
1 TIMOTHY 2:1-2

*T*o experience happiness
in the midst of pain and privation
is clearly a work of God's grace.
It is a paradox to the world.

As sorrowful, yet always rejoicing;
as poor, yet making many rich; as having
nothing, and yet possessing all things.
2 CORINTHIANS 6:10

$\mathcal{W}$e may rejoice
in all of God's blessings,
but we should boast
only in the Lord.

∾

But God forbid that I should boast
except in the cross of our Lord Jesus Christ,
by whom the world has been crucified
to me, and I to the world.
GALATIANS 6:14

*B*ring joy in the night.
Sing a hymn after the lights are out
and everyone is in bed!

Let the saints be joyful in glory;
Let them sing aloud on their beds.
PSALM 149:5

$\mathcal{J}$esus praised His father, God,
and so should we.

∾

In that hour Jesus rejoiced in the Spirit and said,
"I praise You, Father, Lord of heaven and earth,
that You have hidden these things from the wise
and prudent and revealed them to babes."
LUKE 10:21

$\mathcal{H}$appiness is the Lord.

∾

For to me, to live is Christ,
and to die is gain.
PHILIPPIANS 1:21

Other volumes to enjoy in the Moments for Your Life series:

∾

God's Little Answer Book
God's Little Promise Book
Together Is Forever
God's Best for Your Success
The Mirror Our Children See